A+ books

L Is for Lemur

ABCs of Endangered Primates

by Sharon Katz Cooper

Consultant: Chris Smith
Education Manager
Duke Lemur Center, Durham, North Carolina

CAPSTONE PRESS
a capstone imprint

A+ Books are published by Capstone Press,
1710 Roe Crest Drive, North Mankato, Minnesota 56003
www.mycapstone.com

Library of Congress Cataloging-in-Publication Data
Library of Congress Cataloging-in-Publication data is available on the Library of Congress website.
ISBN 978-1-4914-8034-2 (library binding)
ISBN 978-1-4914-8405-0 (eBook PDF)
Summary: Describes endangered primates of the world by assigning
a species or primate-related term to each letter of the alphabet.

Editorial Credits:
Jill Kalz, editor; Bobbie Nuytten, designer; Jo Miller, media researcher;
Katy LaVigne, production specialist

Image Credits:
Alamy: Dan Callister, 29, Nature Picture Library, 5, Reynold Sumayku, 13; David Haring/Duke Lemur Center, 15, 16, 21; Minden Pictures: Roland Seitre, 7, 14; National Geographic Creative: Lynn Johnson, 27; Nature Picture Library: Roland Seitre, 10 (right); Newscom: ImageBROKER/Florian Kopp, 11, ImageBROKER/Siegfried Grassegger, 24, Minden Pictures/Kevin Schafer, 26, 28, Minden Pictures/Thomas Marent, 22, Minden Pictures/Xi Zhinong, 23; Science Source: Terry Whittaker, 10 (left); Shutterstock: Abeselom Zerit, 6, Alexander Mazurkevich, 18, Bildagentur Zoonar GmbH, 17, davemhuntphotography, 1 (left), Emi, 4 (left), Eric Gevaert, 20, grass-lifeisgood, cover (top left), GUDKOV ANDREY, 4 (right), javarman, 12, KAMONRAT, cover (right), Nickolay Khoroshkov, 8, sgar80, cover (middle left), tristan tan, cover (bottom left), 1 (right), Trybex, 9, zuanhuongho, 25; Steve Coombs, 19

Design Elements:
Shutterstock: Hein Nouwens, Ramona Heim

Printed and bound in the USA.
009690F16

Note to Parents, Teachers, and Librarians

The E for Endangered series supports national science standards related to zoology. This book describes and illustrates primates. The images support early readers in understanding the text. The repetition of words and phrases helps early readers learn new words. This book also introduces early readers to subject-specific vocabulary words, which are defined in the Glossary section. Early readers may need assistance to read some words and to use the Share the Facts, Glossary, Internet Sites, Critical Thinking Using the Common Core, Read More, and Index sections of the book.

ENDANGERED!

Endangered plants and animals are at high risk of disappearing. Our planet may lose them forever because of habitat loss, hunting, or other threats. When one species goes away, the loss often hurts other species. All life on Earth is connected in some way.

All of the primates in this book are in trouble. They are either near threatened (at some risk), vulnerable (at more risk), or endangered. Their numbers are small. But they don't have to disappear. You can help by reading more about them and sharing what you learn with others.

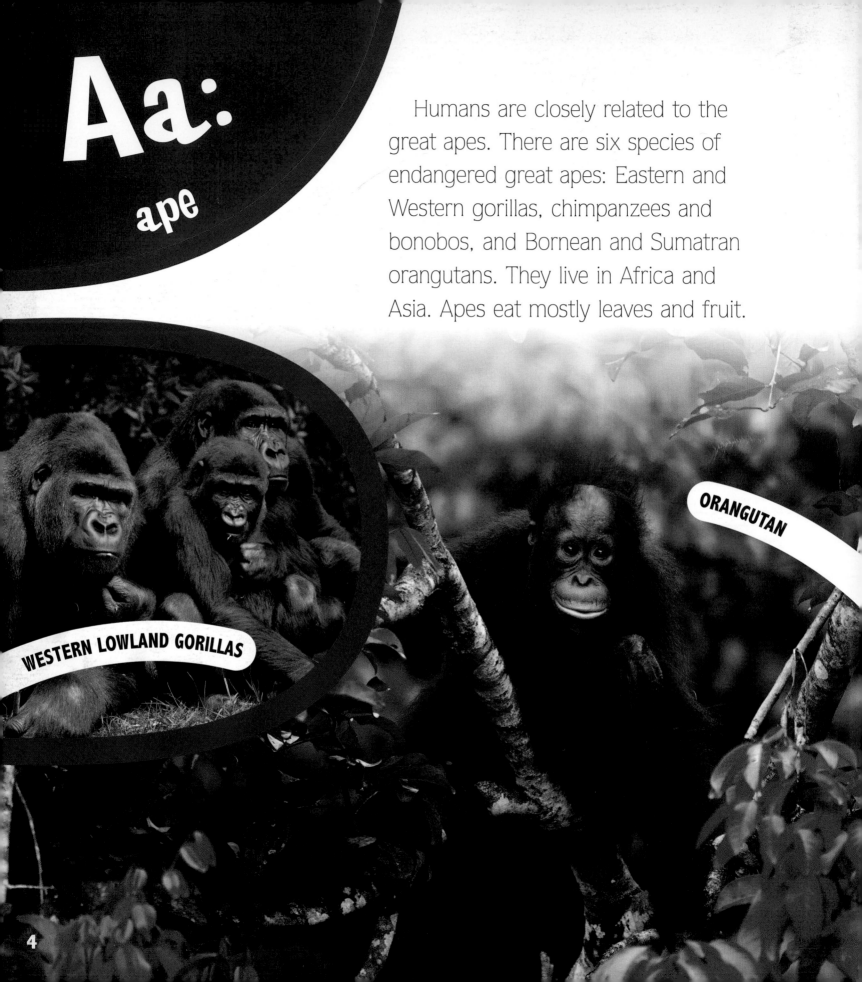

Aa:
ape

Humans are closely related to the great apes. There are six species of endangered great apes: Eastern and Western gorillas, chimpanzees and bonobos, and Bornean and Sumatran orangutans. They live in Africa and Asia. Apes eat mostly leaves and fruit.

WESTERN LOWLAND GORILLAS

ORANGUTAN

Bb: brown howler monkey

Northern brown howler monkeys have very loud calls. They HOWL! People can hear their cries from 3 miles (4.8 kilometers) away. Northern brown howler monkeys live in the forests of Brazil and Argentina, countries in South America. Prehensile tails help the monkeys grip branches.

5

Cc: chimpanzee

Chimpanzees are our closest living relatives. They are part of the great ape family. Chimpanzees live in large groups in African rain forests. They eat fruit, plants, insects, and eggs. They usually walk on all fours (hands and feet). Sometimes they walk upright, like people do. At night they sleep in nests made of leaves.

Dd:
Douc langur (DOOK LANG-er)

Gray-shanked Douc langurs live in the forests of Vietnam, a country in Asia. They have golden faces, white chins, and dark-gray hands and feet. They stand about 30 inches (76 centimeters) tall. Their tails are as long as their bodies. There are only about 700 gray-shanked Douc langurs left in the wild.

Ee:
Eastern lowland gorilla

Eastern lowland gorillas live in the forests of the Congo, in Africa. They eat mostly fruit. Deforestation and war have destroyed much of the gorillas' habitat. Scientists think there are fewer than 8,000 Eastern lowland gorillas left in the wild. It has been hard to count or protect the animals because of the ongoing war in this area of Africa.

Ff: family

Many primates live in family groups of up to 20 animals. In some species, males are the leaders of the group. One male gorilla lives with many females and their babies. In other species, females lead. Lemurs live in groups led by older females. Male lemurs leave the group when they are old enough to live on their own.

RING-TAILED LEMURS

Gg:
golden-headed langur (LANG-er)

Golden-headed langurs (also called Cat Ba langurs or white-headed langurs) are very difficult to find. There are fewer than 70 left in the world. They live only in Asia, on Cat Ba Island in Vietnam. Cat Ba langurs live in the forest. Caves on the island protect them from predators and heat.

Hh:
habitat loss

Habitat loss is a big reason why primates and other species become endangered. People cut down trees or clear land to build farms, roads, and cities. When that happens, animals can no longer live in those places. Animals cannot always move to new places, so they begin to die out.

Ii:
indri (IN-dree)

Indris are the world's largest lemurs. They make very loud calls that sound like singing. The calls can be heard for miles. Groups of indris sometimes sing together, like a choir. Indris can jump as far as 32 feet (10 meters) between trees. They are the only lemurs with short, stumpy tails.

Jj:
Javan slow loris

Javan slow lorises live in Indonesia, on the island of Java. They are active only at night, moving slowly from tree to tree. Poachers often capture and sell lorises as pets. However, lorises do not make good pets! They are venomous. The poison in their bite can be deadly.

Kk:
Kloss' gibbon

Kloss' gibbons live in rain forests on four Indonesian islands. They use their long arms to swing easily from tree to tree. Kloss' gibbons live in groups and are active during the day. A special sac beneath their chin allows them to make very loud calls. Males often sing together before dawn.

Ll:
lemur

Lemurs are native only to Madagascar, an island off the coast of Africa. There are about 100 species of lemurs, and 73 of them are endangered. Lemurs vary in size. Some lemurs weigh as little as 1 ounce (28 grams). Others weigh as much as 20 pounds (9 kilograms).

Mm:
mouse lemur

Mouse lemurs are the smallest lemurs and the world's smallest primates. They range in weight from 1 to 4 ounces (28–113 g). Nearly 20 kinds of mouse lemurs live in Madagascar. Most of them are endangered or vulnerable. They eat both plants and animals, such as small geckos. Their large eyes help them see clearly in darkness.

Nn:
Northern sportive lemur

Northern sportive lemurs are one of the world's most endangered primates. Scientists think there are only about 50 of them left. These lemurs got their name because they stand like boxers. They're sporty! They live only in the northern forests of Madagascar. Northern sportive lemurs are nocturnal. They sleep during the day and look for food at night.

Oo:
orangutan (eh-RANG-eh-tan)

Orangutans are long-armed apes that live on the islands of Sumatra and Borneo in Asia. They grow to be about 5 feet (1.5 m) tall. Their arm span can reach 7 feet (2.1 m)! Orangutans live in tropical rain forests and spend their time in trees. Their name means "person of the forest" in the Malay language.

Pp:
Propithecus candidus
(proh-PITH-i-cuss CAN-dee-duhss)

Propithecus candidus is commonly known as the silky sifaka (shee-FAAK). Sifakas are large lemurs that live only in the northeastern rain forest of Madagascar. Long, soft fur gives the animals their silky name. "Sifaka" comes from the lemurs' call. It sounds like *shee-FAAK* repeated several times.

Qq: quickly dropping numbers

Habitat loss and hunting can shrink primate numbers quickly. It can take years for the numbers to increase. Many primate species have only one or two babies every year, or every few years. Orangutans, for example, have babies only every eight years. At that rate it could take a long time for the group to return to a healthy size.

RED-BELLIED LEMURS

Rr:
red ruffed lemur

Red ruffed lemurs live in only one small part of northeastern Madagascar. Their thick red fur protects them from rainy and chilly weather. They use a special claw and the toes on their back feet to brush themselves. Most lemurs have only one or two babies at a time. Red ruffed lemurs have up to six babies at once.

Ss:
spider monkey

Spider monkeys live in rain forests in Central and South America. They use their long prehensile tails to swing from tree to tree. They live together in groups of up to 24 animals. As their name suggests, spider monkeys look like spiders climbing through the trees. And sometimes, spider monkeys eat spiders too!

Tt:
Tonkin snub-nosed monkey

Tonkin snub-nosed monkeys have an upturned "snub" nose, eyes rimmed in blue, and thick pink lips. For a long time, scientists thought these monkeys were extinct. But in 1992 a small group of them was discovered in a forest in Vietnam. Only about 200 Tonkin snub-nosed monkeys are alive today.

Uu:
unlawful hunting

Many countries have laws against killing or trapping endangered animals. But some people break the laws. They hunt primates for food or medicine. They capture them to sell as pets. Conservation groups work with governments to try to stop unlawful hunting. They show local people new sources of food and medicine. They teach them why the endangered animals should be saved.

Vv: Vietnam

Vietnam is a long, narrow country in Southeast Asia. It is hilly, with thick forests. Many endangered primates live there. Deforestation is a huge problem in Vietnam. It is quickly destroying primate habitats. People from around the world are working with the Vietnamese people to save the primates' homes and protect this country's natural beauty.

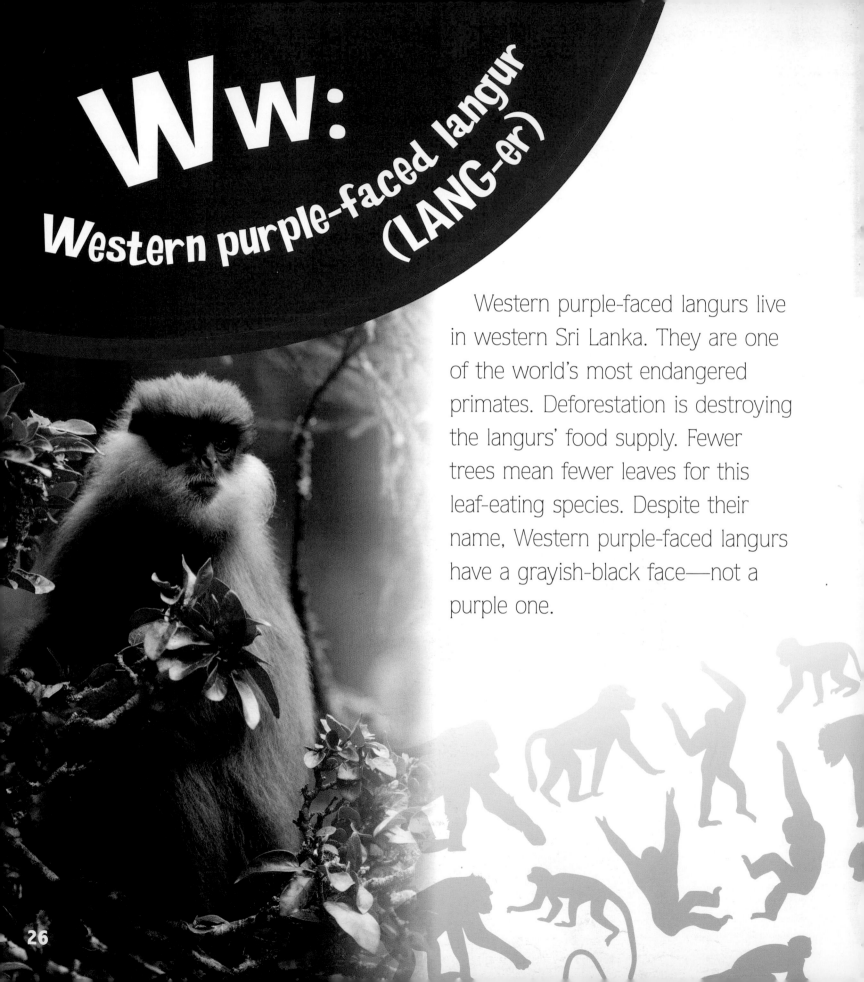

Ww:
Western purple-faced langur (LANG-er)

Western purple-faced langurs live in western Sri Lanka. They are one of the world's most endangered primates. Deforestation is destroying the langurs' food supply. Fewer trees mean fewer leaves for this leaf-eating species. Despite their name, Western purple-faced langurs have a grayish-black face—not a purple one.

Xx: exotic pet trade

Some primates are endangered because people capture them to sell as pets. This is not legal in most places, but it happens often. Illegal hunters make a lot of money—billions of dollars each year—from selling these animals. Primates do not make good pets. They are wild animals that should remain in the wild.

Yy:
yellow-tailed woolly monkey

Yellow-tailed woolly monkeys live in the Andes Mountains of Peru, a country in South America. Chocolate may be one reason why yellow-tailed woolly monkeys are endangered. Chocolate is made from cacao tree seeds. When people clear land to grow cacao, the monkeys' habitat disappears. The monkeys have nowhere to live, and they start to die out.

Zz: ZOO

Many zoos keep groups of at-risk primates and help them produce babies. Some of the young animals may one day return to the wild. Zoos also teach visitors about at-risk primates. They show them ways to help. The Bronx Zoo, for example, runs conservation programs in Africa. It also offers classes about primates at its park in New York.

SHARE THE FACTS

- Orangutans use large leaves like umbrellas to protect themselves from rain.

- Common brown spider monkeys can have blue eyes, just like some humans.

- The word "lemur" comes from a Latin word that means "ghosts." People gave them this name because of their large eyes and because many species are active at night.

- Scientists believe lemurs arrived on the island of Madagascar millions of years ago, traveling across the water from Africa by raft.

- There are more ring-tailed lemurs in captivity in the world than any other species.

- Lemurs have a row of teeth on their bottom jaw that acts like a comb. Called a tooth comb, it's used for grooming their fur.

- Slow lorises are the world's only venomous primates.

- Male gorillas can grow up to 6 feet (1.8 m) tall and weigh up to 600 pounds (272 kg).

- The **Duke Lemur Center** (*lemur.duke.edu*), in Durham, North Carolina, holds the world's largest collection of lemurs outside of Madagascar. The Center studies and protects lemurs and offers many educational programs to the public.

- Organizations working to protect endangered primates include **Primate Conservation, Inc.** (*www.primate.org*), the **Jane Goodall Institute** (*www.janegoodall.org*), the **African Wildlife Foundation** (*www.awf.org/wildlife-conservation/mountain-gorilla*), and the **Endangered Primate Foundation** (*www.endangeredprimate.org*).

GLOSSARY

conservation—the protection of plants, animals, and natural resources such as water and soil

deforestation—cutting down trees until a forest is destroyed

endangered—at risk of disappearing forever

extinct—when a species no longer exists on Earth

habitat—a place where an animal can find its food, water, shelter, and space to live

near threatened—could become endangered in the near future

nocturnal—active at night and resting during the day

poacher—a person who hunts illegally

predator—an animal that hunts and eats other animals

prehensile—able to grip or grasp

primate—any animal in the group of animals that includes humans, apes, and monkeys

protect—to save from danger

species—a group of plants or animals that share common traits

venomous—able to produce a poison called venom

vulnerable—at high risk of becoming endangered

INTERNET SITES

FactHound offers a safe, fun way to find Internet sites related to this book. All of the sites on FactHound have been researched by our staff.

Here's all you do:

Visit *www.facthound.com*

Type in this code: 9781491480342

Super-cool stuff! Check out projects, games and lots more at www.capstonekids.com

CRITICAL THINKING USING THE COMMON CORE

1. Name three reasons why a primate species may become endangered. (Key Ideas and Details)

2. Find a photo in this book of a prehensile tail. Explain how a primate may use it. (Craft and Structure)

3. Why do you think most primates have brown, black, or gray hair? (Integration of Knowledge and Ideas)

READ MORE

Friesen, Helen Lepp. *Chimpanzees*. Amazing Primates. New York: AV2 by Weigl, 2016.

Gagne, Tammy. *The Most Endangered Animals in the World*. All About Animals. North Mankato, Minn.: Capstone Press, 2015.

Throp, Claire. *Lemurs*. Living in the Wild: Primates. Chicago: Heinemann Library, 2012.

INDEX